At Your Service

Home Remedies

Lindsey "Mo" Morris II

authorHOUSE®

AuthorHouse™
1663 Liberty Drive
Bloomington, IN 47403
www.authorhouse.com
Phone: 1-800-839-8640

First published by AuthorHouse   8/24/2011

ISBN: 978-1-4634-1830-4 (sc)
ISBN: 978-1-4634-1829-8 (hc)
ISBN: 978-1-4634-1828-1 (e)

Library of Congress Control Number: 2011910113

Printed in the United States of America

Contents

About The Author

Lindsey Morris II, Author of At Your Service Home Remedies has done it again by writing another book that everyone needs and can use in their homes. In this book, he has come up with ways to make life easier when doing the day to day cooking, cleaning, laundry, and miscellaneous things around your entire dwellings. Not only that, he has come up with ways to save you money at the fraction of the cost from supplies you already have in your homes. To make it even more worthwhile why you should have this book is, it's affordable, there's not one out there like it, or compared to it that makes life a lot easier by cutting down the time in doing inside and outside work whereas you can use the time elsewhere, like spending it with the ones you love or just resting enjoying the day. Furthermore, I would say in getting this book would be an ideal gift for all to have and not just for today, but also for those who are becoming new home owners for the very first time. Lindsey Morris attributes much of his success in writing this book to the many places he has traveled and lived around the world and that one day the world will come to know and use the same remedies in their homes as he did, even today.

Introduction

Have you wondered to yourself or asked close friends for ideas of preserving the freshness of foods after you've purchased them? How about after you've prepared and cooked them? Have you ever sought delicious ways to improve on leftovers or simply to enhance the flavors of food by using spices and seasonings never used before? How about when it comes to mixing and measuring those seasonings and ingredients you've never used? Would you like to know what seasonings blends well with what, to produce healthy meals that will bring your family back to the table? How often have you had to stop in the middle of a meal preparation because you did not have the proper kitchen utensils at your service, hassle free? How about our dieters? If you're like me, most of you are familiar with and excited about dieting and loosing extra pounds, but you also want to experience the same great taste in foods, without all the saturated fats, calories, and a host of other unmentionable preservatives, right? And just when you think dinner's done, there's always one last thing that will require your immediate attention… House Cleaning! Yes, house cleaning, that squeaky kind of clean that can take up much of your day without the proper cleaning solutions. Solutions that can clean everything in your household including that difficult stain on clothes or carpeting, including the oil on the floor of your garage. If any of these questions have caught your attention, then this book is designed for you. This book is intended to make your housework easier, by placing simple household remedies right at your fingertips.

CHAPTER 1
Food

Grocery Shopping 101

Coupons: A newspaper on Sunday can turn into major savings in coupons. Get to know your local grocery retailers. Many offer double or triple coupons on certain days. This can add up to double-digit savings on your grocery bill.

Read the ADS: Sunday grocery ads are filled with great weekly sales, especially on meats and produce.

Freeze: When meats go on sale, stock up! You should never pay full price for your meat unless you use a specialty butcher.

Plan Ahead: Plan out your meals for the week in advance. Studies have shown that shopping daily results in extra impulse buying and 20-30 % increases in your grocery spending.

Make A List: Stick to your list! Avoid those "impulse" items.

Leftovers: Stretch your ingredients by using leftovers.

Adults: Never go to the Grocery store hungry (especially children).

Missing an Ingredient

Almond Extract: Use Amaretto

Brown Sugar: For each cup: use 1 cup granulated sugar mixed with 1 tablespoon molasses

Buttermilk: For each cup: mix 1 cup of plain yogurt or sour cream mixed with ¼ cup skim milk (use only 1 cup of the mixture)

Cake Flour: For each cup: measure 1 cup of all-purpose flour, remove 2 tablespoons and replace with 2 tablespoons of cornstarch

Chili Sauce: For one cup: combine 1 cup tomato sauce, ¼ brown sugar, 2 tablespoons vinegar, ¼ teaspoons cinnamon, dash of ground cloves and dash of allspice

Chives: Use green onion or scallion tops instead

Cornstarch: (for thickening sauce) for each tablespoon: use 2 tablespoons all-purpose flour

Corn Syrup: Replace with honey

Cream of Tartar: for ½ teaspoon: use 1 ½ teaspoons of lemon juice

Ground Red Pepper: For ¼ teaspoon: use 8 drops of Tabasco (or other hot pepper sauce)

Pumpkin Pie Spice: For 1 teaspoon: combine ½ teaspoon cinnamon, ¼ teaspoon ginger, 1/8 teaspoon allspice, and 1/8 teaspoon nutmeg

Shallots: Use red onion

Sour Cream: Use plain yogurt

Tomato Sauce: For a 15-oz can: combine a small can of tomato paste with 1 ½ cups of water. Mix well!

Unsweetened Chocolate: (melted) for each ounce: use 3 tablespoons unsweetened cocoa mixed with melted butter or margarine

Vanilla Extract: Use brandy

Whipped Cream: Chill a 13-oz can of evaporated milk for 12 hours. Add 1 tablespoon lemon juice. Whip until stiff

Wine: For ½ cup: use ¼ cup of wine vinegar (red or white wine vinegar depending on what the recipe calls for) mixed with 1 tablespoon of sugar and ¼ cup of water

Low –Fat Ingredient Substitutions

Bacon: Canadian bacon, turkey bacon or lean ham

Butter: Reduced-calorie margarine or margarine made with safflower, soybean, corn, canola, or peanut oil

Chocolate, unsweetened (1 oz): 3 tablespoons unsweetened cocoa plus 1 tablespoon margarine

Cream Cheese: Nonfat or light process cream cheese, Neufchatel cheese

Egg (per egg): ¼ cup egg substitute or 2 egg whites

Fudge Sauce: Low fat chocolate syrup

Ground Beef: Ground turkey

Ice Cream: Nonfat or low fat frozen yogurt, sherbet or sorbet

Oil: Safflower, soybean, corn, canola, or peanut oil in amount reduced by One-third

Sour Cream: Yogurt

Whipped Cream: Whipped evaporated skimmed milk (chilled)

The Healthy Fast Food Pantry

Lots of Fresh Fruit: Always have apples, bananas and oranges. Add seasonal fruit like peaches, melon, grapes, pears, cherries, and nectarines.

Lots of Fresh Vegetables: Always have carrots, green peppers, cucumbers, onions, celery and lettuce. Add seasonal vegetables or vegetable on sale like winter squash, sweet potatoes, broccoli, asparagus, zucchini, green beans, snow peas, and tomatoes.

Low-Fat Cheeses: Have a variety, such as skim milk mozzarella, low-fat cheddar, cream cheese, and cottage cheese.

Yogurt: Get both plain and flavored yogurt

Canned Beans: Stock up on chick peas, black beans, refried beans

Milk or Soy Milk: Aseptically sealed tofu and temper; eggs (hard boiled); peanut butter; pasta; pasta sauce; small cans of tomato sauce for pizza; seasoning like mustard, soy sauce, mayonnaise,; bread; tortillas; tuna and salmon (canned); variety of ready-to-eat whole grain cereals; instant plain oatmeal; dried fruit, especially raisins; honey; soups (low-fat); boxed macaroni and cheese; bagels; muffin mixes; frozen vegetables; granola bars; graham crackers; fig newtons; rice cakes; 100% juices; chicken; and potatoes both white and sweet potatoes and yams.

Handy Measurement Conversions

3 teaspoons=1 Tablespoon

4 Tablespoons= ¼ cup

5 Tablespoons+ 1 teaspoon = 1/3 cup

8 Tablespoons=1/2 cup

16 Tablespoons=1 cup

1 cup=8 fluid ounces (1/2 pint)

4 cups=32 fluid ounces (1quart)

16 cups=128 fluid ounces (1 gallon)

Cooking

Bacon: When cutting up bacon for frying, freeze it first and it will cut. If you coat your bacon in flour before you cook it your bacon will not shrink as much.

Baked Potatoes: Want a Baked Potato with Oven Baked Taste but that's cooked in your microwave faster than lightening? Clean potatoes and poke holes in them. Get as many grocery bags as you have potatoes and put one potato in each bag. Place bags in microwave... 6-8 minutes for one potato, add 5 minutes for each additional potato. I usually only cook two at a time and cook 2 for about 15 minutes, but check them about 5 minutes before done. Use an oven mitt and squeeze the potato to see how soft it is. If it is soft enough you're done. All the moisture from the bag puts it back into your potatoes. NOTE: THE STEAM FROM THE BAG IS VERY HOT WHEN OPENING THE BAG AFTER COOKING, BE CAREFUL AND ALWAYS BE SAFE.

Baking: Substitute apple sauce for vegetable oil in exact amounts. It contains less fat.

Baking Pies: When baking a pie with filling, first bake the crust for 10 minutes then add in the pie filling and bake as usual. This will make the crust crisper and less soggy.

Bananas: Freeze over-ripe bananas until you have enough to make a bread or cake. They will turn black in the freezer and they will be very mushy but they are great for baking. Be sure to freeze them in the peel.

Beans: When cooking dry beans, such as red beans or any type of dry beans, place in a microwavable container and cover with water. Microwave on high for 30 minutes to start. While you're doing this, you can prepare onions and whatever type of meat you choose to season beans. After all the water has been absorbed by the beans, I usually add just enough water to the beans and microwave them again until the beans are soft followed by placing some sausage in an ovenproof pan covered with bacon. Then I cook it in the oven until bacon is crisp. By the time your beans are rehydrated, the meat is cooked and ready to add to your stock pot. Then season as usual. There is no difference in the taste and you can cut the cooking time by an hour or so.

Boiling Eggs: If you put a lot of salt in the water the eggs will shell perfect every time. Place a few drops of vinegar in your water when boiling eggs. If an eggs cracks it will not spill out into the water. Bring eggs to a boil, turn burner off leaving on top of stove for 15 minutes. Pour water off and ice along with very cold water, let cool and they will peel so easy. Let the water come to a hard boil, stick a pin in the large round end of the egg, drop it in the water, and cook it for 5 minutes, turn the water off and let them stand for 10 minutes. Then put in ice water, the shell slips right off.

Boiling Over Pots: Place a wooden spoon across the top of the pot when boiling water. It separates the steam and keeps it from boiling over. To keep boiling potatoes or noodles from running over, rub butter on rim of pan.

Bread Crumbs: Need Italian seasoned breadcrumbs? Toast old bread (center loaf or the ends). Leave for a few minutes to get hard then tear in little pieces in blender. Add garlic powder, oregano, and onion powder, any other seasoning you want and blend until crumbled. Put in freezer bag. It's keep for up to 6 months.

Buttermilk: If you are out of Buttermilk, in a glass measuring cup, try mixing 1 tablespoon of regular vinegar and add fresh milk (low-fat or whole milk)

to equal 1 cup of your made up buttermilk. Add 1 teaspoon lemon juice per 1 cup, of milk (regular or low-fat) to make buttermilk. Add two tablespoons of white vinegar to one cup of whole milk. Mix well and let set for 5 minutes to let milk thicken.

Cake: To make a cake lower in cholesterol (whether is homemade or from a box mix), simply use egg substitute or egg whites instead of whole eggs, and applesauce instead of vegetable oil. The cake will still be delicious and it's better for you. Applesauce is especially good in spice cake and carrot cake. To grease a cake pan, etc., use a paper towel to dip into the shortening. This will spread easier and make cleanup faster.

Cake Moistener: To make your homemade cake moister, use about a half-cup of sour cream (or less) along with it. You don't taste it at all, it just makes it super moist, but watch out; moist cakes tend to fall apart easier. Mix 1 tablespoon of miracle whip into the batter.

Chicken: Want an easy way to remove skin from chicken? Use a paper towel. Grip the chicken firmly with the paper towel and pull the skin off. The paper towel works like magic and clings right to the skin. Now you can have healthier chicken for you and your family. Before you put your chicken pieces on the grill, pre-boil them for about 20 minutes. Makes for quicker, juicer grilled chicken. Freeze the broth for chicken soup later. Add onion, carrots, celery, and rice. An "effortless" meal.

Chopping Food Safely: When chopping vegetables or meat, lay a damp towel under the cutting board to prevent it from sliding around.

Coffee: To keep coffee from getting into your pot (automatic coffee pots) just wet the rim of the coffee filter with your fingers and stick it to the filter.

Coffee Creamer Substitute: Use Powdered Milk in coffee instead of Creamer, it will mix easier and taste great. Plus it is cheaper so you can add as much to coffee as you would like without feeling guilty.

Cooking Oil Substitute: Out of cooking oil simply replace it with miracle whip.

Cooking Spray: I have been cooking for 25 years and until a year ago; I just did not discover the convenience of cooking spray. Now nothing sticks and it is useful in so many ways, like spraying the cover of yeast breads and rolls, cake pans, even cooking burgers and meats that you don't want a lot of grease in. I cannot be without this item and thought maybe there is another old time cook out there that has just not tried using the spray. Trust me; it is a wonderful time saver.

Cornmeal and Flour Bug Repellant: Place a bay leaf or two into your flour and cornmeal containers. The bay leaf will repel bugs and will not leave a funny taste when cooking.

Cookies: Refrigerate cookie dough prior to baking to prevent the cookies from spreading and going flat.

Corn on the Cob: When boiling corn on the cob, add a pinch of sugar to help bring out the corn's natural sweetness. When boiling corn on the cob, add enough milk to just cloud the water. This keeps the corn from sticking to your teeth.

Cornbread: When making cornbread by the mix, if you're out of milk, substitute powdered coffee creamer and water instead. This also works with pancake mix. When making cornbread, if you're out of milk, substitute a can of cream style corn. Not only does it work in a pinch, it also tastes really good. Out of eggs when making cornbread? Add a heaping Tablespoon of miracle whip or Mayonnaise.

Cream Substitute: Use heavy cream when making cream based sauces. You also can use cream of mushroom soup to thicken a cream base sauce. If too thick, thin with a little milk.

Deviled Eggs: Instead of spooning the filling into the eggs, which is time consuming and messy, fill a zip lock bag with the filling, cut the corner off and then squeeze onto the eggs. No mess, no fuss; when you're done, toss it in the garbage. You can use it with cake icing to decorate cookies and cakes too. If you deviled egg filling is too runny add some dry instant mashed potatoes-it will thicken them and add no taste.

Dough: When rolling out pie dough, biscuits, etc., dampen counter top and then cover it with plastic wrap. Dampening it will prevent the plastic from moving and when you're finished; you can just roll up the plastic wrap and throw it away. No mess! When cutting out dumplings I always use a pizza slicer instead of using a knife it's much faster and lots of safe fun for children.

Fish: After cleaning fish that has scales, soak fish in water with little vinegar (about 2 capful in a half sink of water). This will get rid of the slime and the fishy smell. Proceed with seasoning.

Fried Foods: To stop your grease from burning simply cut the top of an onion and add to your grease upon putting in a skillet or pan. Grease will never burn. If you like your eggs over easy but the yolk breaks, try this instead; after the clear part of the egg starts to turn white, put a little water in the pan and put a lid on it until it covers the yolk. No more busted yolks.

Egg Salad: When making egg salads use a potato masher instead of a knife to mash/cut up the eggs. It is a lot faster and less messy.

Egg Substitute: If you don't have enough eggs to bake a cake substitute those with a little miracle whip. It works and you can't taste it at all. For Eggs in baking use Ener-G egg replacer, ½ cup banana, applesauce or silken tofu.

Gravy: When making thickening for gravy, use half flour and half cornstarch. Your gravy will not lump. When making gravy, use instant mash potatoes, just add flakes to hot boiling broth and stir briskly, instead of cornstarch or flour.

Grease: To remove burnt grease and seasoning from pan, add baking soda then vinegar then hot water. Boil for 10-15 minutes. Scrub with scouring pad.

Grapes: Cleaning grapes is a snap when you use white vinegar. Fill your sink or large bowl with cold water. Add about ¼ cup of white vinegar. Add grapes to the water and gently move them through the water for about 1 minute. Let grapes sit about 5 minutes in water. Remove and drain on clean towel. The vinegar cleans and removes all dirt and residue from the grapes. They are fresh and clean with no vinegar smell or taste. It works well on apples, oranges, pears, and all vegetables.

Ground Beef: Don't rush around when you need ground meat for dinner. Cook up a large batch when it is on sale and put it (drained) in zip lock bags, in the freezer. When you need it in a hurry, a little or a lot, just break in into sections or use more than one bag.

Graham Cracker Crust: When making graham crust pie crust, crush the crackers using a rolling pin in a zip lock bag. Add melted butter and sugar to the bag and then close. You can work the ingredients together in the bag without having to wash another bowl or get your hands dirty.

Hamburgers or Meatballs: Keep your hands wet with water and the meat won't stick to your hands. Makes for much easier cleanup. Before you make hamburgers, wash your hands with Dawn and the meat will not stick to your hands.

Hamburgers Patties: Use an upside down (or lip side up) sour cream or cottage cheese lid under a sheet of wax paper to make hamburgers patties. The edges of the lid help keep the patty round and when cooked, they are about the size of the hamburger bun.

You can still make them as thick or as thin as you like, but they will be bun sized. When cooking cheeseburgers this works great, place cheese in the burger then with turner simply place cheeseburger upside down on the bottom bun making the cheese next to the bottom bun, then add condiments the top bun comes off clean and the cheese stays undisturbed under the meat patty and makes for easy assembly. When cooking hamburgers on the grill or anywhere, make a hole in the middle of the burger with your finger. The meat will cook evenly and the hole will close up, no more pink hamburgers.

Hard Boiled Eggs: If you have hard-boiled eggs and get them mixed up with your fresh eggs, just spin then like a top. The hard-boiled eggs will spin and the fresh ones won't. Shake salt in water when boiling eggs. If they crack, they will not spin into the water. If you want to peel an egg without tearing up the whites, after cracking the shell, start on the most rounded end of the egg, use a teaspoon and gently lift the shell. Rinse and use as you wish.

Hot Pepper Burn: Apply olive oil and you will have no burning feeling.

Ice Cubes: If you need to make ice in a short period of time, fill ice tray cubes with warm water. The warm water freezes at a much faster rate than if you filled them with cold water. We use a lot of Ice Cubes in the summertime and when it is hot they melt fast. I now use Cup Cake tins to make my ice cubes and they last so much longer and don't take as many to fill a glass.

Ice Cube Substitute: Cut lemon up in pieces and freeze in a bag. Place the lemon pieces in a glass with water for a healthy glass of lemon water. Also you can use frozen pieces of lemon like ice cube.

Lasagna: Soak lasagna noodles in cold water for 15 minutes. After all other ingredients are ready to assemble, remove noodles and pat dry with paper towels. This softens the noodles somewhat and reduces the cooking time for the lasagna to half.

Leftovers: Keep two large plastic ice cream buckets in the freezer, one for leftover poultry and cornbread and one for leftover roast beef and vegetables (such as corn, carrots, etc). When full, make cornbread dressing with the first and homemade soup with the second. Small piece of onion or celery can go into either container.

Lemon Juice Substitute: If you don't have lemon juice, I use a tiny bit of lemon Kool-aid. Instead of lemon juice use ½ of lemon extract.

Lettuce: When cleaning lettuce, turn head of lettuce upside down and hit core against counter or table and then pull core out. Run water through the head of lettuce to wash it thoroughly and then turn upside down again to drain. Never use a metal knife on lettuce; this will turn the lettuce brown. Using a plastic knife to shred or cut lettuce will keep the lettuce looking fresher.

Measuring: Save the measuring spoons and syringes from children's medicines. They are better than teaspoons for liquid like vanilla or other extracts.

Meat: I sometimes work late, so when I thaw out meat for supper, I thaw meat on the lower refrigerator rack for 2 or 3 days and cook them all at one time. I then only have to prepare a quick vegetable, stemmed cabbage, carrots, can veggie, or salad to accompany it each day.

Meatloaf: I shop for meat at a store where I buy in bulk. When I make meat loaf I make two or three and put one in the oven and the other one or two I freeze for a later time. The day before I'm ready to bake one I take it from the freezer and put in the fridge so it can thaw, then the next day I bake it some carrots and potatoes all in the same pan, and there you have a good hot home cooked meal with hardly any prep time.

Milk Substitute: Use non-dairy coffee creamer mixed in water for recipes that call for milk. This is great for people that are allergic to dairy products.

Nacho Cheese: When serving nacho cheese in a crock pot, use a roasting bag in the crock pot before putting the cheese in. Afterwards, lift the bag out and throw away. The cleanup it will be a breeze.

Non-Sticking Noodles: When cooking pasta, put a cap full of vegetable oil in the water before adding the pasta. Your noodles won't stick together.

Oil Substitute: When a cake recipe calls for margarine or oil, you can use applesauce as a substitute. It works great and less calories.

Onion Hands: Do you have onion smell on your hands after cutting one? Use the metal part of a knife or spoon and rub your hands with it while under running water. After cutting an onion, spray vinegar on your hands as well as on your cutting board and knife. The strong odor will completely be removed. To remove onion smell from your hands, use a half-teaspoon salt in your palm. Dampen it with a few drops of water, dishwashing liquid and rub it all over your hands as you would soap. Rinse and the smell will be gone. If you have an onion that is hard to peel, because the skin is dry, just drop it in some water for about 5 minutes. When slicing an onion, to avoid tears, try holding a piece of white bread in your mouth while slicing, it prevents tears every time. When chopping onion, you will have fewer tears if you put you chopping board under the exhaust fan on your stove or light a candle and place it near the cutting board. Before slicing an onion, place onion in the freezer for half hour. This will keep the onion from smelling and burning your eyes. To prevent tears when cutting an onion, cut the root end off last.

Tears: To make chopping onions a less teary-eyed experience hold two unlit matches in your mouth. Have the non-striking end in your mouth. No tears on your cutting board. Place the onion in the microwave for a few seconds and then chop it up. You won't tear up anymore.

Opening Jars: To get the lid off a jar, slide a butter knife under the lid and twist the knife. It will break the seal and the lid will come off easy.

Orange Zest: To always have some orange zest on hand just save your peels and freeze them. Then you will always have some on hand.

Pasta: Boil water first then add pasta, bring to second boil and stir, then cover. Then shut off stove. DO NOT LIFT LID! IN 7 MINUTES IT SHOULD BE DONE! SAVES GAS OR ELECTRICITY.

Peanut Butter Cookies: To make the criss-cross pattern, instead of using a fork tine, use a potato masher. It's easier to handle and one print will go the width of the cookies.

Pie Crust: Using a graham cracker crust? Brush it with a raw egg and bake for 10 minutes at 350 degrees. Let cool before filling. When you cut the pie the crust will stay intact and not crumble.

Popcorn: To assure all grains will pop store popcorn in refrigerator prior to popping.

Pudding: When cooling pudding, pie filling etc., put clear wrap on top of the mixture before cooling in the refrigerator. The wrap must be in contact with the complete surface area of the mixture. No more gooey film on top of your pudding.

Raw Egg Clean-up: If you drop a raw egg, simply pour salt on it, this makes it easier to clean up.

Rice Krispy Treats: To spread these bars easily into the pan after preparing, run your hands under cold water for a few seconds. Wipe excess water off your hands, and press the rice krispy mixture into the pan. Repeat cold water if necessary.

Clogged Salt Shaker: Place about a tablespoon of uncooked rice in a shaker then fill the rest of the way with salt. The rice will absorb the moisture and keep the shaker from clogging.

Sauce: If you put too much salt in a sauce, drop in a potato while the sauce is simmering and it will absorb much of the salt.

Soup: Don't throw away the bones from that chicken you had last night, boil the bones with a little chopped up onion and celery (don't forget the leaves) salt and pepper to taste. You have a great chicken stock for soup, veggies and rice.

Squash: To slice squash into, first microwave for about a minute or so depending on the size. Once that is done, it slices easily and the seed removal will be much easier.

Stop Boiling Over Pots: To keep pots from boiling over when you boil potatoes or pasta, just spray pot with Pam first. Your stovetop will thank you.

Sweetened Condensed Milk Substitute:

1 cup powdered milk
1/3 cup Boiling water
2/3 cup Granulated sugar
3 tablespoons Butter (optional)
Place all ingredients in blender. Blend until sugar is dissolved. Equals approx. 1 can sweeten condensed milk.

Taco Shells: Lay the whole stack of them directly on the oven rack while they're still inside one another (you can leave the little "cushion insert" in the very first one) and heat them they hold their shape a lot better leaving more room to put all the goodies inside.

Tastier Cakes: When cake mix calls for water use buttermilk instead. It will make the lightest and best cakes. Plus it will give it that homemade taste.

<u>Toaster: Always unplug your toaster after use. Toaster is the #1 cause of house fires!!!</u>

Tupperware: To keep tomato stains out of your plastic bowls when storing tomato-based dishes, spray bowls first with cooking spray.

Vidalia Onion Substitute: Want a sweet onion for your hamburger and Vidalia's aren't available? Cut a whole yellow, white, or red onion in half and soak in a bowl of cold water (1 cup or to cover with ¼ cup of sugar added). Let soak at least 15 minutes, this really sweetens the onion and takes out the bitter bite. The longer they soak the sweeter they are.

Wine: Do you have leftover red wine from cooking? Fill the red wine into ice cube trays or small ice cube bags and put it in the freezer. That way you don't have to open a new bottle, every time you need red wine for your cooking. In a pinch you can substitute beer in place of wine for a recipe that calls for white wine. I usually double the amount of beer to wine and reduce to desired thickness of sauce.

Food Freshness

Baked Goods: To keep cakes, cupcakes, doughnuts, or any bread/ bakery products fresher longer, put a small glass/bowl of water in the box and close the lid. The water keeps the items moist, so that they are not "crunchy".

Bread: Put your bread in the fridge and it will keep fresh well past the date.

Brown Sugar: Put a piece of bread in brown sugar to keep it soft.

Butter: If you "stock up" on butter, keep the excess in the freezer and it will keep longer.

Celery: Before putting in refrigerator, wrap celery in aluminum foil and it will keep for weeks.

Cereal: If you usually have several boxes of cereal opened at one time. The best way to keep them fresh is to roll the bag down several times and then pinch it closed with a pinch clothespin.

Champagne: To keep champagne bubbly after opening and serving the first glass, place a spoon handle, or a fork handle, whichever fits into the neck of bottle and your champagne will remain bubbly even until the next morning to serve at breakfast. It works!

Chilies: To keep green chilies fresh, take off the stem, wrap them in a paper towel and keep in a Ziploc bag. I have had chilies fresh for a month.

Cookies: Place a slice of bread in with your fresh baked cookies, or even after they've gotten a little harder than you desire. It will keep the cookies soft or soften them up.

Cottage Cheese: To keep the unused portion of cottage cheese from becoming "soupy", replace the lid tightly and store UPSIDE DOWN in your refrigerator.

Crackers: Store an open sleeve of crackers in an empty Pringles can to keep them fresh longer.

Crackers: Put them on a cookie sheet and bake at 200 degrees for about 15-20 minutes. They will be fresh again.

Cucumbers: To keep cucumbers as fresh and firm as the day you bought them, simply wrap each one in a paper towel and store them as usual in your vegetable crisper. They can last up to three weeks.

Keeping Produce Fresh: How to make just about everything in the refrigerator stays fresh longer. After it is opened just store it upside down. I have tested this with Milk, Sour Cream, Dip, Applesauce, Jelly, Jam, Pickles, Peppers, and more. If you can't store it upside down "milk for instance" store it on its side just make sure that the liquid covers the cap. When storing anything upside down try to make sure that the contents sink to the "Top" to create a seal". The reason this works is bacteria needs to "land" on food and needs air to flow. This method stops both.

Frozen Goods: Put an ice chest with some ice in your car the next time you go grocery shopping, and ask the bag person to put all the cold and frozen items together in the bags, so you can fit them in the ice chest for the ride home, especially in hot weather. The food will keep much longer without having been subjected to the heat, even for a few minutes.

General: I use the packages of clothes pins you can buy for a dollar or two to use to close bags of chips, cereal, bread, left over cake mix and multiple other things.

Grapes: When washing and cleaning white or red grapes for later consumption, place in Ziploc bags and store in freezer. When the urge for something sweet hits you, help yourself to this great healthy snack.

Fruit Salad: Sprinkle fruit salad with lemon juice, pineapple juice or plain pineapple to prevent it from turning brown.

Lettuce: To keep a head of lettuce fresh, completely wrap it in a paper towel and put it in a zip lock bag. I have had lettuce last over a month.

Potato Chips: If you have a bunch of potato chips bags open simply roll them up and throw them in the freezer. This will keep them fresh a lot longer.

Mushrooms: To keep mushrooms from spoiling quickly, keep them in the carton and cover with plastic film wrap. Puncture the plastic wrap with a fork about five times. Refrigerate. Mushrooms will stay fresher and slime-free longer if you store them loosely in a brown paper bag (lunch bag type) in the refrigerator.

Onions: Got leftover onions (or any similar vegetable)? Just chop them up in the food processor, and then freeze in ice cubes trays. After frozen, dump the frozen veggies into a freeze-safe plastic bag. Now you can easily use the "ice cubes" for cooking or adding to recipes; and the good part is you don't have to chop anything up and you can use only the amount you need.

Potatoes: Put an apple (any kind) in your store bought potatoes bag. The apple will keep them from sprouting.

Salt and Sugar: To help keep your salt and sugar from getting moist and clumping, place a saltine cracker in the container with it. The cracker soaks up all the moisture and your salt and sugar will stay fresher, longer.

Strawberries: To keep strawberries fresh, store unwashed berries, stems on in a closed jar. Wash and stem when ready to eat. They will keep up to a week.

Vidalia Onions: If you want to keep Vidalia onions throughout the winter, put them in a knee high panty hose and place them in the bottom vegetable tray in your refrigerator.

Vegetables (General): Wash vegetables such as lettuce, carrots or peeled onions, let them dry and place in a sealed zip-lock bag with a dry clean paper towel. They will last until all is used with no discolored leaves or bad spots. I have found that fresh veggies keep for a very long time in the Tupperware "fridge smart" containers…I have had them to last for three weeks and grapes have lasted over a month.

Chapter II
Cleaning

Chapter 19

Cleaning Bathrooms

Bath Tubs/Shower and **Sinks:** For built up hard water stains in your toilet or any porcelain surface, use a pumice stone. It won't scratch the porcelain and it works in a sink for tough stains.

For those really stubborn bathtubs stains/rings use carburetor cleaner. Just spray it on (be sure your bathroom fan is on or a window is open for ventilation) and wipe off immediately. Repeat if first application isn't 100% successful.

Use any shampoo on a wet cloth and wipe the tub or sink clean. Do not use shampoo with conditioner added.

For soap scum in the tub or shower, I've found that "Greased Lightening" works wonders! It can be bought at Lowe's or Wal-Mart. Just spray it on, leave set for about 10 minutes, and then wipe off with a sponge or rag. This is wonderful cleaner for other areas of the house too.

To remove soap scum from the tub use Mr. Clean Vanishing sponge with Dawn dishwashing liquid and you don't scrub just wipe across and it's unbelievable you have to see it for yourself.

A used dryer sheet is good for cleaning your bathroom sink and tub. Just get it wet and clean away. It also leaves a nice shine. It also takes away that ring around the tub.

For bath tubs simply use oven-cleaning spray. Leave on for about 10 minutes. Be sure to use the oven spray that is unscented and be sure to ventilate the room while cleaning (the fumes are toxic.)

Bathtub ring that will not come off with bathtub cleaners will easily come off with Mr. Clean Magic Eraser; this will clean almost anything with little effort.

To remove soap scum from showers doors and bathtubs, use a mixture of baby shampoo and water in a spray bottle. A fine mist trigger works best. Use one capful of shampoo per bottle and fill the rest with water. It works really well on mirrors that may have buildup.

When your shower is dry spray furniture polish on it, then wipe. It reduces the built up on soap scum.

The scrubby gloves that you find in the health and beauty department are great for cleaning the shower (just make sure you use a different set for bathing!)

After cleaning your tub and shower walls, apply a coat of car wax to keep mineral deposits from hard water along with the soap from accumulating on the surface. This will make it easier for your next cleaning. Be sure to wear rubber slip protectors on your feet as the tub will be very slick.

Bathroom Caddy: Hang a shoe bag with pockets in it on the bottom door brushes, blow dryers, curling irons, extra soap, shampoo, etc...

Counters: To have extra sparkle on the bathroom counters, rub turtle Wax on and buff off. Water will not leave spots either. Apply twice a year for best results.

Extra Shine: Windex makes your bathtub, faucets, and sink shine after cleaning them. Just spray it on and wipe off with a soft towel or paper towel for a beautiful shine.

Faucets: To make your faucets look brand new. Get a tube of V-05 hair oil and rub it on the faucets with a towel. Then buff to a perfect shine.

Glass: After you clean the glass, spray regular Pledge on and buff lightly. The water rolls right off and you don't have to clean the glass as often.

Hair Spray: Use warm pure white vinegar to clean hair spray off your bathroom floor.

Metal: Put shaving cream on faucets and other metal items in your bathroom and you will be delighted with the shine. To make chrome faucets really sparkle and shine wipe them down with isopropyl rubbing alcohol.

Mildew/Mold: Mix two tablespoons of dish detergent and one pint of bleach in a spray bottle. Spray it on the area in question and the mold or mildew will disappear and not come back for a while. It can also be sprayed on tubs, showers when camping, and on the north side of the house where the green mold likes to grow from not enough sunlight.

Mirrors: Spray a small amount of shaving cream on mirrors and wipe off with a paper towel. This will keep mirrors from steaming up for approximately 406 weeks. For streak mirrors, clean them with clear rubbing alcohol. Use old cotton tee shirt to wipe the mirror clean.

Rust Rings: If you get orange water spots on your tubs or sinks don't spend tons of money on CLR or other iron and rust removers that don't work well. Just grab your tube of toothpaste. Make sure you use the paste kind and not the gel. I have found that the cheap "grainy white kind" works best. Simply wet the area a little bit then squeeze a generous amount of paste over the area and rub it in, then use an old tooth brush to brush away the stains. For stubborn stains, add more paste and some baking soda, and then let it soak for about 5 minutes then scrub it off.

Shower Curtains: To clean soap scum off you shower curtain liner, wash it in vinegar using a couple of towels in the washing machine. Then hang dry.

To clean mildew off your shower curtain, use baking soda on a damp cloth or brush.

To clean mold from shower curtain liner, remove and soak in the tub with water and bleach for a few minutes. Rinse in clear water and re hang to dry. This method cleans the curtain instantly and disinfects at the same time.

Put your shower curtain with a little bleach and warm water in your bathtub while cleaning the rest of the bathroom by the time you're done it's done too. Just hang it back up and use the bleach water to clean your tub.

To remove mildew and water stains from your plastic curtain, put in your washing machine, on hot, and add 1 cup of bleach, when done hang outside to dry! Not only do you get the water stains off, you have killed any germs in the process.

Shower Doors: After cleaning glass shower doors or the tile, coat them with Lemon Oil furniture polish. This makes them shine like new. It will also remove any soap scum left on glass as well as soap scum left on tile or metal in the shower or bath.

Try using liquid cascade dish soap. Pour the liquid all over your glass shower doors and then scrub the glass with a paper towel or cloth. Do not rinse with water until you have cleaned the whole door. Also replace the paper towels after 3 or 4 scrubs then rinse with water and pat dry. You will have the cleanest shower doors in the world.

To get hard water deposits off of plastic use liquid fabric softener. The cheaper the better.

Spray on "Avon's- Skin So Soft" with soft towel or paper towel… Leaves doors sparkling and bathroom smelling great.

To prevent hard water stains on shower doors, spray with WD-40 after cleaning.

Soap Scum: Mix together white vinegar and lemon juice. Spray down your bathtub, and then sprinkle it with baking soda. Scrub the soap scum and other stains away.

Tiles: After cleaning soap residue from your tiles, rub them down with RainX. The RainX helps to repel the soap scum for a longer period of time and you will be cleaning those tiles a lot less often.

Tile Grout: Never have to clean mildew again. Seal your tile grout. SurfaceGard Penetrating Sealer can be found at Home Depot and it's guaranteed to last for 20 years. It's easy to apply too. Just paint it on with a sponge brush. It's invisible and it works.

Toilet Bowl: Use denture tablets to take care of those rings inside toilet. Just drop two tablets into toilet bowl and it will leave your toilet fresh and clean.

Pour a can of Coca-Cola into the toilet bowl and let it sit for about an hour. Then flush it clean. The citric acid in Coke removes stains.

If you have a nasty stain around your toilet. Clean it with a pumice rock.

Put two tablets of Alka Seltzer in the toilet once a week to help keep it clean. This really works.

Windows: Wash inside panes one way (vertical) and the outside panes the opposite (horizontal.) That way you know which side isn't clean or has streaks.

Mix cornstarch and water together in a bowl and wipe on windows with a cloth. Take a clean, dry cloth and wipe the window clear. This will remove dirty film from your windows and they will be crystal clear.

The easiest and quickest way to get sparkling windows, at

approximately $1.00 a gallon is your auto windshield washer solution. Spray it on and wipe with a paper towel. Cheap, easy and clean. To make your windows really shine, after cleaning them rub them down with crumbled newspaper.

Cleaning Adhesives

All Purpose: Rubbing alcohol will remove sticker glue from most anything.

Try using De-solve-it (a citrus solution) it can be purchased at Wal-Mart and is great for removing adhesives such as stickers. It also works great for removing chewing gum from hair and shoes.

If you can't get a label off of anything, spray sticky paste with WD-40 and wipe away.

Adhesive Labels: Coat the label with oil; leave it overnight to break down the glue. Peel off the next day; clean the oil with dish soap and rinse.

Peel label off and rub with baby oil. The rest of the sticky goo should come right off.

Spray Oust sanitizer on a paper towel to wipe off sticky glue residue from stickers.

Glue on Glass: Use WD-40. It wipes the glue right off without scrubbing. After it is removed, run back over the spot with a wet paper towel and the excess WD-40 will wipe off.

Tape: Use baby wipes and the sticky residue will come right off, especially from tile.

Gum: To remove gum try the product "Oops." It can be found at Wal-Mart in the hardware section. Just put it on a paper towel and gently rub it into the area with gum on it. It only takes a few seconds and the gum completely disappears.

To remove gum, pour a small amount of Pine Sol onto the gum and it will start to dissolve the gum when you rub it between your fingers. You may need to let Pine Sol set on gum that has been there for a while. Also it removes gum from hair. You might want to test it in a spot that wouldn't be noticeable first.

For gum in your hair try using cooking oil. Put it on a washcloth and rub the oil on the gum. Remove the large part of the gum first then gently remove the rest.

Fast Orange or Goop hand cleaner dissolves gum from hair. Just spread it on and let sit. When you shampoo hair it will just wash out, it completely dissolves.

For gum stuck to carpet, clothes, or hair use a can of compressed air. Use the kind used to clean computers. Turn the can upside down and spray a quick squirt to freeze the gum. Then remove it. Be careful not to spray on skin because you could get "frost-bite."

Price Labels: Remove price labels by coating the label with several coats of white vinegar. Let the vinegar soak in and after several minutes the label will rub off.

I use peanut butter to remove the sticky mess left behind on glass from price stickers. Just rub a spoonful of peanut butter on the mess and leave for a couple of hours and then wash off.

To remove adhesive left from removing price tags etc. apply a small amount of Avon Skin So Soft oil spot to the spot, rub lightly with your finger, and let set a couple of minutes. Use a rag or paper towel to wipe it off. Works great on all gummy residues left on objects.

Sticky Substances: Use lighter fluid to take off all sticky substances such as gum or adhesive labels.

Tree Sap: Peanut butter is great for removal of tree sap.

The product "Oops" will remove many sticky substances off of windows, mirrors, and many other things. This product can be found in the cleaning supplies Department.

Cleaning Carpet

Candle Wax: Carpet or other fabrics) Cover the spot with a brown paper bag or old cloth and run a hot iron over the bag. Keep moving the bag to a dry part of the bag until all of the wax has been absorbed. The wax comes up immediately and won't harm your iron.

Carpet Cleaners (machines): Using club soda in the carpet shampoo-er cleans as well as if not better than carpet shampoo and does not leave the soapy residue behind. And, yes, it will get out most spots.

After steam cleaning your carpet, rinse using fabric softener in your water. Your carpet will feel softer and if you use a lot of the softener it will help prevent spills from soaking in.

Carpet Deodorizer: Save money on Carpet deodorizers, mix any ground spice, I use cinnamon, and baking soda. Sprinkle on carpet and then vacuum. Also get Mr. Clean shine on your floors, add vinegar to your mop water and you will have shiny floors. This is what the advertisers use in their commercials.

General Cleaners: Wash an old cleaner bottle and fill it with hot water, then squirt in about 5 seconds worth of dish soap, cap and close. The great thing is this cleans stains on carpets, counters, etc.

One part vinegar to 2 parts water is the best and safest way to clean your linoleum floors. If you have a soap residue build-up left behind this will dissolve leaving the linoleum free of spots.

Gum Removal: Use an ice cube. Put the ice cube on the gum until the gum is hard. Then remove the ice, and the gum.

Spray the gum with W-409 and let sit for 3 minutes then scrape off with a butter knife.

Fresh Spills: Don't ruin a towel by blotting it up. Heavily pour table salt on the spill, let it soak up the spill. When it draws it up then use a dustpan and scoop up salt. Use seltzer water with a drop of detergent to finish up the cleaning.

The perfect way to get fresh Chocolate Milk out of light colored carpets is a product called Simple Green. It is non-toxic. Just use it full strength, even though it tell you to dilute it. Then clean the carpet. It is all gone. It also works great on the stove to remove the grease build up.

Indentations: If you have Indentations in your carpet after moving the furniture use ice. Rub an ice cube in the indentation and carpet will pop right back up.

Oil Stains: For oil or tar on your carpet, clean it with rubbing alcohol.

Red Wine: Immediately pour a small amount of white wine over the red wine to neutralize the "red" color of the wine. Take a white towel and blot all of the white and red wine up. Next get a clean white towel and dampen it with a little water. Place the damp towel over the area where the spill was and step on it a few times. Then place down and step on a dry towel until you have absorbed all of the moisture (may need more than one towel).

Dab the excess up immediately and be sure you do not rub the stain. Take approximately 1 teaspoon of Oxi-Clean (approximately 2-3 oz.) and mix it in luke warm water. Shake to dissolve the Oxi-Clean then squirt it on the stain (the stain should turn blue.) Then take a clean cloth and dab stain if still remains repeat.

Stains: Windex will remove almost any stain you have. It has removed red Kool-Aid from beige carpet, burgundy hair dye from a baby blue shirt and, worst of all, blood from white wind pants. Just spray Windex on the stain rub gently and throw it in the washer or use a cool damp cloth to wipe away.

Or

Denture tablets dissolved in water will remove stains from carpet and clothing (even old stains.)

Or

To remove most stains from your carpet. Use a clean white cloth with Isopropyl Alcohol (standard household use type) use a lifting motion on the stained area and the stain will vanish. You should test first in an area not noticeable to make sure it doesn't damage your particular carpet. Once your stain is gone, vacuum to fluff up the area.

Or

Use a 3 to 1 mixture of vinegar and water to remove most any carpet stain.

Or

Spray bathroom cleaner Scrubbing Bubbles on carpet stains. Allow it to set for a minute then wipe clean.

Or

I have found out that using Huggies Baby Wipes (regular) will take most any stain out of carpets, new or old. It's really great!

Or

To soak up just any spill including soda juice drinks pour salt to absorb the liquid.

Urine: A 50/50 mixture of white vinegar and water takes out urine smells out of carpets and furniture when pets have accidents.

Cleaning Methods/Carpet

There are two primary methods of carpet cleaning: dry cleaning and hot water extraction. Consult with a reputable carpet cleaning company to determine which is the best method for your type of carpet. Some brands of carpet may also recommend the best or only method to be used.

Carpet Dry Cleaning

Dry cleaning utilizes chemical cleaning solutions to extract dirt. There are three dry-cleaning methods:

1. **Dry Foam:** A shampoo is applied to your carpet, allowed to dry, and then vacuumed up, bringing the dirt with it.
2. **Dry Chemical:** After a cleaning solution is applied to the carpet, a machine spins a large bonnet from side to side to absorb dirt in the carpet. After the bonnet is saturated with dirt, it is replaced with a new, clean bonnet and the process continues.
3. **Dry Compound:** An absorbent mixture resembling wet sawdust is spread over the carpet. A machine brushes the mixture into the carpet to absorb the dirt. When the mixture dries, it is vacuumed out, taking the dirt with it.

Hot Water Extraction

This carpet-cleaning method is also known as steam cleaning. Hot water extraction forces a hot water based cleaning solution into the carpet under high pressure, and then sucks it back out of the carpet along with the dirt.

1. **Portable Extraction:** The carpet is cleaned by a small

machine using hot tap water and powered by the electricity source in the house. Typically rented to do-it-yourselfers, some professionals also use portable units.

2. **Truck Mounted Extraction:** This uses a large cleaning machine mounted on a truck or van. The water is heated to a higher temperature and is shot into the carpet at a higher velocity than is possible in portable machines.

Many carpet-cleaning professionals believe this is the most effective way to clean mostly because the heat kills the bacteria and the extra power separates dirt. These powerful machines also pull most of the water back out of carpets, leaving them damp but not wet, and able to dry much quicker.

Cleaning Floors/Walls

Cob Webs: To clean walls of cob webs and dust use a dust mop just for this chore.

Crayon Stains: Using Baby oil removes crayon from any surface. Apply a little at a time and gently rub. Brings it right out.

Or

Put a little WD-40 on the wall and wipe with a cloth or a paper towel and the stain is completely gone.

Or

To clean crayon marks off tables and walls use a little after shave. Wipes it right off. Ideal for those that have small children that love to display their artwork anywhere or those that work in the childcare industry.

Crayon: This tip is very handy for those who have young children whom enjoy expressing their love of art on painted walls. WD-40 will take crayon off painted walls. Spray it on the masterpiece and wipe off with a soft cloth, afterwards wipe the wall with warm soapy water to remove any greasy spots.

Or

Use a damp cloth dipped in baking soda. Comes off with little effort, just a little elbow grease that's all.

Or

To get crayon marks off a wall, use toothpaste (not gel) with a cloth and rub on the spot until the mark is gone. Then use a damp cloth to wipe the dried toothpaste away.

Hardwood Floors: To get hardwood floors looking great mix 1 part Windex to 4 parts water then clean. You can also use 1/3 cup of white vinegar in a half gallon of luke warm water. The vinegar helps the water evaporate quickly to keep spots from appearing.

Heel Marks: To remove black heel (patent leather shoe) marks from floors, simply spray with hair spray and wipe clean before it dries.

Linoleum Floors: Putting two capfuls of baby oil in your mop water can help leave your linoleum floors looking bright and shiny without you having to buy expensive products on TV.

Mark on Walls: If you have crayons marks, or paint scuffs on walls, use the New Mr. Clean Magic Erasers. They are wonderful for patio furniture as well. There are no chemicals in the cleaner but they do have slight abrasive, but will not scratch walls.

Or

To clean cigarette smoke or anything else off the walls use Mean Green. Mix half water with half Mean Green.

Or

Antibacterial hand sanitizer is very good for removing ink, crayon, and other marks on walls.

Mark on Floors: The easiest and fastest way to get rid of those stubborn black heel marks on floors is to erase them. All you have to do is take an eraser and just erase them. This works because I've tried everything I could possibly find to use and none of them worked and it only takes a few seconds to do.

Or

To get rid of those black marks on the floor rub them with your feet wearing white cotton socks.

Or

Use a sneaker with a white sole and rub it back and forth over the mark. The friction gently removes the mark. Another way remove those black marks are to rub them once or twice with a tennis ball. The ball is easy to hold and works well.

Or

Use Styrofoam to erase them. An old Styrofoam cup works great as well panty hose, it will wipe right off.

For "gunk" that builds up around the outer edge of the kitchen floor, I use "Greased Lighting". Spray the "gunk" and let it sit for about a minute or so. The "gunk" wipes clean with a towel.

Cleaning Kitchen/Food

Appliances: To keep your stove top clean and shining, use a good car cleaner wax on the painted surface around the stove eyes. Just apply as you would to your automobile. Clean up is a breeze after the heaviest cooking. This can also be used to clean the fronts of most appliances except for stainless steel.

Baby Bottles: To clean milk residue out of baby bottles, put a tablespoon of raw rice, one drop of dishing washing liquid and hot water in the bottle. Fill the bottle up half way with hot water and shake it up for about 2-3 minutes. Of course this is only done after the sterilizing of bottles stage is over.

Baking Dishes/Pans: To remove burnt-on food from baking dishes/pans, place a dryer sheet in the bottom and fill with hot water. Wait about ½ hour and it should wipe clean. May have to be repeated if really messy.

Burnt Food on Pans: Use baking soda, dish washing powder, and hot water. Then use a scrub brush.

Burnt Food: Place an unused dryer softener sheet into your cooking vessel that has dried or burnt on food. Add hot water soak overnight.

Sprinkle dishwasher soap to cover most of burned food, add just enough water to let it soak. Add more later if needed, soak overnight and scrape out food with plastic scraper.

Clogged Drains: For slow moving drains, such as kitchen sink slowed by grease, pour one bottle of hydrogen peroxide, let sit for 10 to 15 minutes. For real slow drains, you may need to use 2 bottles.

Coffee Cup: I have found that using a baking soda paste gets rid of coffee and tea stains in my coffee cups.

Coffee Pots: Forgot and left the glass coffee pots on the heating element and now you have burnt coffee in the bottom of your pot? Just put crushed ice in the pot along with some salt and swish it around.

To clean it if has set on the warmer too long, take some rice and add a little bit of water to it. Stir around for a few minutes and it should clean. It might take more than one try.

To clean a pot once you have burned coffee in it, put ice salt and squeeze some fresh lemon juice into the pot and let it sit for awhile or even over night, then clean out. A little lemon juice and salt also works to get grime off of the coffee pot burner too.

Cooked on Food: (on the sides of a slow cooker) Simply fill the pot with warm water, drop in 1 or 2 denture cleaning tablets, let sit over night. Makes for easy clean up the next morning.

Copper Pots and Pans: Use Tabasco hot sauce to clean the bottom of your copper pans or any copper. Let sit for awhile and it will come clean and look like new.

Counter Tops: To remove ink, Kool-Aid, and other stains from counter tops, use a paper towel soaked in a little rubbing alcohol and it will come right off.

To clean stubborn grease on the stove top after cooking or baking, spray a little bubbling bathtub cleaner it will cut right through the grease and leave it sparkling clean.

Use Windex to take fruit punch stains off of counter tops and tables.

For burn marks on tables and counter tops, rub spot with toothpaste.

Crock Pot: When using a crock pot to cook in you can line the crock pot with an oven roasting bag let the bag hang over the sides so you can still get the lid on and stir as needed. After you finished cooking you just remove the bag and the crock pot is clean. Discard the bag and contents in the trash for less mess.

Disinfectant: Keep rubbing alcohol in a spray bottle. Use it on any surface that you would normally use window cleaner on. Not only does it clean but it will also kill germs.

Dishwashers: To clean your dishwasher use one package of Kool-Aid Lemonade, run it through a wash cycle and it will come out clean and smelling great.

To get the muck off of washing machines in the undersides of lids use salt and squeeze lemon juice over the top of the salt. The salt aids as an abrasive while using a toothbrush to get into those hard to reach places. Makes sure you rinse with water when finished, it takes off the paint if left on too long. So be very careful when doing this.

For cleaning iron deposits from dishwashers, Tang drink powder works well. Just fill the detergent section with Tang and run it through its regular cycle.

For Burnt on Glass Cookware: Simply sprinkle it with Oxi-Clean and fill it with hot water. Let stand for an hour or more. Then clean the stuck on food will come right off.

If you burn a cobbler, use 1/3 sheet of fabric softener and water and soak for several hours or overnight. You will be amazed at how easily you can clean the dish. This will work on any dish where sugar burns during baking.

Garbage Disposal: To clean a garbage disposal, run ice cubes and oranges or lemons through it. Use the juice first.

After running hot water and baking soda in the disposal, drop a few drops of vanilla down your drain for a pleasant smell.

George Foreman Grill: After you finish cooking on it, wet two paper towels with hot water, fold them together long wise, place on grill and close lid. Wipe off all food in minutes.

Grill Racks: When cleaning the racks on the grill, crumble a piece of aluminum foil and scrub the cool racks with the foil. This works really well because it gets inside the small slots on the racks.

Melted Plastic: If a plastic bread wrapper is left to close to your toaster the plastic melts onto the appliance, you remove it by rubbing it off with WD-40.

Microwave: I put a large bowl of water inside the microwave with some baking soda (not too much) and a few drops of real lemon juice. Cook for 1-2 minutes, let sit for 20 minutes. Take a clean rag and clean it. Stuck on things comes right out, and the lemon gives it a nice clean scent.

For burnt popcorn in the microwave, first clean real good with vinegar water, then stuff with newspaper for 24 hours. Paper will absorb odors.

The next time you clean your microwave run some water in a bowl with just a little bit of dishing washing liquid. Bring to a boil, the steam from the water makes the microwave wipe clean. You must use dish washing liquid it will not work with water alone.

Wet a kitchen sponge and squeeze out the excess water. It needs to be wet and not soaked. Put it in the microwave for 1-2 minutes. When the microwave is finished take out the sponge. It will be very hot. Set aside.

Then take a dishcloth or paper towel and easily wipe away the food that was stuck on. This not only helps you clean your microwave, but the heat also get rids of bacteria in your sponge.

Microwave Splatter: Use a new coffee filter to cover foods cooked or heated in the microwave to control splatter.

Oven Racks: Put about 2 cups of Ammonia in a plastic bag along with the racks. Seal it up tight with a twisty and leave it over night or all day. You can wash them easily with no scrubbing.

Plastic Containers: Don't throw away stained plastic containers. Just place them in direct sunlight for at least four hours.

Pots and Pans: For foods stuck in cooking pots and pans, use a bit of dish soap and water in the pan, put on stove and bring to a boil. Food will come right off.

Putting a coffee filter in your iron skillets will keep them from rusting.

Refrigerators: When cleaning out your refrigerators add baking soda to your cleaning water. It will help minimize odors for a longer period of time.

Sinks: Put a coat of car wax on your kitchen stove and bathroom sinks and they are a breeze to clean up after messy little hands and cooks.

If you want your kitchen sink to shine like new after every time you wash the dishes, dry the sink with a dry towel and then wipe it with a newspaper. The ink from the newspaper will make it shine and look new.

Thermal Coffee Pot: To clean, simply put approximately a teaspoon of Oxi-Clean into the pot and fill with hot water. The residue will float to the top.

Tupperware: To keep tomato-based foods from staining plastic bowls, spray the bowls with Pam non-stick food spray before using.

To get stains out in Tupperware try the new Cascade Plastic Booster it works well.

Wax Candles: Out of Holders: Put a little water in the bottom when adding a new candle. They slide right out, even after the water evaporates. You may have to break into pieces due to size but makes it easier. Wash the holder before starting new candle because you can get build up on the glass from the water.

The easiest way is to place the candleholder in the freezer for about an hour and remove from freezer and the wax will pop right out.

White Glass Stove Tops: I use to have a gas stove top that had a white glass top. I tried all the best grease cutting products and all of them left an oily film. Then I tried my own cleaner, mixed with ½ cup of white vinegar and a ½ cup of water which I put in a spray bottle, works great and cost nothing.

White Kitchen Sinks: Use a little liquid dishwashing detergent and take a brush and spread around and rinse. Whatever stays continues to bleach the surface. Looks great even a little better.

Cleaning Household

Broken Glass: To pick up small slivers of broken glass from a hard surface, use a slice of bread. Place the bread on the broken glass slivers and press down gently. The glass will stick to the piece of bread and not into your fingers.

Blinds: Fill your bathtub with hot water adding Bleach Powder Cleaner to the water. Place mini-blinds in the water and soak until the dirt rinses off easily.

Computers: To easily clean your computer and keyboard use baby wipes. You will be amazed at how much dirt they actually pick up.

Every Day Mess: Baby wipes are a nice easy way to clean up everyday messes. They can be used for dusting, polishing shoes, and cleaning car dashboards.

Dusting: If I'm short on time, I put on a pair of white cotton gloves sprayed with furniture polish. Makes it easy to dust all those little nick knacks as well.

Dryer sheets works great when dusting nick/knacks and around them. Also good for dusting TV screens, stereo, and other electronics.

Dust Mites: Getting rid of dust mites will help improve allergies. Do this by vacuuming your mattresses and washing bed sheets once a week in hot water. Also, don't forget to wash curtains and blinds that collect dust.

Fresh House Scent: Buy an air freshener of your choice and stick it behind your vacuum bag. When you vacuum it will make your house smell good.

Furniture: If you are out of furniture polish, you can use Armor

All or Formula 2000 on your tables and counters. Also can be use on stainless steel for a bright shine.

Or

Wash with warm water and dishwashing liquid. Be sure to dry furniture very well with soft dry cloth. By using this method, dust collects slowly.

Or

If you leave a drink on the coffee table and get a watermark, take mayonnaise and rub into the wood. It is like new again with a shine.

Or

To remove water marks from wood furniture use toothpaste. Just rub the spot with toothpaste on a soft cloth. It doesn't take long, the spot is gone and the luster is back.

Or

To get ballpoint pen out of fabric, spray it with hairspray.

General Stains and **Cleaning:** To remove blueberry stains from clothing, mix milk and vinegar together. Make sure it's a little runny. Soak overnight... you will be amazed.

Or

Totally Toddler is a great stain remover. You can purchase it at Wal-Mart.

Or

Lye soap works well for cleaning kitchen sinks, bathroom fixtures, and clothes that need bleaching. It works really well on heavy soiled work clothes.

Or

The best all-purpose cleaner I've ever tried; I found it on the back of a bottle of ammonia about 13 years ago. It's now call Beth's cleaning solution.

1 cup ammonia
½ cup distilled vinegar
¼ cup baking soda
Mixed into 1 gallon warm to hot water

I keep it in a spray bottle in my kitchen to clean and polish my stove top.

Iron: To clean the bottom of your iron sprinkle ironing board with table salt and then iron over salt with warm iron.

Plexi-Glass: To clean plexi-glass windows use white vinegar and a soft cloth.

Permanent Marker Stains: Use a pencil eraser or hairspray. This really works and comes right off.

Pet Hair in Blankets (and rugs): Toss in the dryer and set it on the Air setting with a large piece of netting (available at fabric stores).This also works to clean stuffed animals that are dusty.

Rusty Spots: Use Mr. Clean Erasers. A few wipes and they are gone. They are also good at cleaning storm doors.

Rust Stains: Kiss those rust stains and mineral deposits goodbye. Use Bar Keepers Friend on porcelain sinks, stainless steel, and fiberglass materials. It's cheap and available at Wal-Mart. It comes in a yellow/blue can and is found by the toilet cleaner section.

Spider Webs: Use a Swiffer mop and a dry sheet to clean hard-to-reach corners.

Tree Sap: To remove pitch from your hands, spray your hands with hair spray and rub them together.

TV Screens: Use cling-free dryer sheet to clean television and computer screens. Simply moisten them and wipe-off the screen.

Wallpaper: Wipe walls with a Swiffer mop and a wet Swiffer pad. It is really quick and so much easier than hand wiping your walls.

Washing Machines: To keep washing machines clean and to remove excess soap that remains in all those holes. Once a week add 1 cup of vinegar to your wash cycle. Be sure to use the hot water option.

Windows: Coffee filters work great for cleaning glass and mirrors. Use with any window cleaner. They're cheap and go a long way.

Or

Wipe the inside of your windows down with shaving cream. It will keep them from fogging up.

Equal parts rubbing alcohol and water makes a great window cleaner at a fraction of the cost of others on the market.

Cleaning Metal/Jewelry

Brass: Use regular white toothpaste.

Or

To get brass shiny, clean it with ketchup and a soft cloth. It brings the shine right out.

Or

To clean brass quickly and effortlessly dip in full strength ammonia for a few minutes then dry. This will not work on coated brass; must be solid brass.

Copper: Want to shine up your old copper and brass lamps or decorative pieces? Put it in the sink, spray with Kaboom, let it set for a few seconds, then rinse and wipe dry. It will be pretty and shiny again. Extremely dirty pieces will require a second spraying.

Copper-bottomed pots: Make a paste of salt and vinegar and rub it on, then wash off with warm water.

Diamonds: To clean diamonds, use baking soda and an old toothbrush make them look like new.

Gemstone Jewelry: Use Vodka and a toothbrush.

Do not use ammonia on gold or any other jewelry, it crystallizes the metal and makes it more prone to crack/break. Especially on prongs

Boil a cup of water in the microwave. When water is boiling put the cup in the sink and add Mr. Clean (about 2 teaspoons). Do not put Mr. Clean with water in microwave, it will make a mess.

Put in jewelry and within 15 minutes it looks new. Do not put pearls, opals, or emeralds in this, they will crack. Rinse with water when finished.

If you have jewelry that is dull, and lost its spark, take 1 to 2 denture tablets dissolve in water, add jewelry and watch the spark and shine come back to all your dull jewelry and it won't harm the jewelry, try it.

Stainless Steel: To remove water spots on stainless steel, rub the area with a clean, soft cloth dampened with white vinegar. Then wipe dry to avoid spots. To clean your stainless steel sink use automatic dish powder.

After cleaning your stainless steel, make it shine with chrome polish by rubbing it on and letting it dry. Once dried, buff with a clean cloth. Also works really good on marble shower walls.

To make stainless steel cookware shiny and clean, put about a tablespoon of white vinegar and enough water to cover soiled area and let sit in a hot pan or simmer while you clean up the kitchen. Wash and dry.

To clean up grease off stainless steel, use a Mr. Clean Magic Eraser. It rubs off without scratching.

Sterling Silver: Polish silver in a pinch by using any non-gel toothpaste. Simply cover the sterling silver with a coat of toothpaste, buff and polish.

Or

You can clean sterling silver with cigarette ashes and water. Rub on the ashes and rinse them off.

Or

Mix water, liquid clothes softener and salt in the sink. Lay a piece of aluminum foil (shiny side up) in the bottom. Dip silverware in and voila polished silver. Sometime it takes quite a bit of salt but works great.

Cleaning Cars

Bugs: When bugs are smashed onto the front of your car dip a dryer sheet in some water to clean them off your car. It takes them right off. Use De-mineralized water; it is great for removing bugs from vehicles along with water spots. Also works great for cleaning windows.

To keep bugs from getting on your car during the season, wash your car well then spray it with Pam or any other cooking spray. The smashed bugs will wipe or wash right off. For removing bugs from the front of your car, use an old knee high stocking when cleaning the car or wet your car first and then spray a little bit of 409, let sit and then the bugs will wipe right off.

Icy Windows: After cleaning car windows on the outside. Put rubbing alcohol on a paper towel and rub over the windows. When warming up the car, if there is any ice or frost on the windows; it will help it to melt it away.

Interior: When cleaning the interior of your car, use Murphy's Oil soap on the vinyl (such as a cover). It looks great and smells good.

To keep the interior of your vehicle smelling fresh/clean, place one or two fabric softener dryer sheets anywhere inside your vehicle overnight-just open/unfold the sheet and stuff one corner into the back of one of the front seats, or any other nook/cranny. This works well for almost any other small contained area in your vehicle, R.V., boat or your home.

Tar: Use peanut butter to get tar off of the exterior of your car.

Tires: Spray white wall tires with Mean Green and gently brush grime away easily. This product can be found at almost any store that sells cleaning products for automobiles.

Chapter III
Garments

Laundry

All Purpose Laundry Stain Remover: For Kool-Aid, blood, chocolate or just any sort of stain, buy a small bottle of the original Dawn liquid dish soap. Apply it and if possible let it set overnight. Wash it the next day and all traces of the stain will be removed.

Or

Simple Green: I use this on all laundry stains. It is much cheaper to buy than the stain removers in the grocery store. Just spray it on a stain and then throw in the washer.

Or

You can use Prell shampoo to remove stains like grass, blood, etc. on clothing. Just rub it in good before you throw the item in the washer.

Or

To remove stains of all kinds, even red mud, just use Windex with ammonia.

Or

To get out tough stains of almost anything use Ajax Dish Liquid (Orchard fresh smells the best). Pre-treat the area with a moderate amount and let it set for about 5-10 minutes then wash inside out.

Or

Spray 409 on clothes stains then wash.

Or

A product called Gonzo that can be found at any cleaning supply store takes out every stain I have tried so far. It has no harmful odor and is kind to the hands. Just rub it in and wash as usual.

Blood: Remove it with hydrogen peroxide. Just wet the stain with cold water then pour the peroxide on the material then rub it together. Let it set (do not let it set on some fabrics or colors). If it doesn't come out before your eyes repeat the procedure until it comes clean. You can also use a soft bristle toothbrush if needed. Be careful with silk and cashmere. Afterwards wash with cold water and detergent.

Or

Regular table salt will soak up blood without damaging most fabrics. If the satin is dry, wet the area with a moist paper towel and sprinkle salt directly onto stain. Be careful not to scrub very hard on delicate fabrics. If the bloodstain is still wet, pour salt directly on and use a moist paper towel to pick up the salt. Repeat until blood is gone.

Or

To get blood out of almost anything use coca-cola.

Colors: To avoid colors from running on new clothing, just soak in cold water and one-half cup of salt for 30 minutes. Works every time.

Fabric Softener: Out of dryer sheets? Take a small palm size kitchen sponge and place in a Tupperware container and pour in your liquid fabric softener to fill 3/4. Put the top on container and allow sponge to absorb softener a few minutes. Take sponge and place in your dryer instead of a dryer sheet. You will not find a better scent when you open your dryer.

Fruit Stains: Pour a quart or more of boiling water from a desired low height onto the stain as the garment rests in the sink.

Golf Shoes: The new Mr. Clean Eraser works great for cleaning the grass stains and ground in dirt off of golf shoes.

Grass and Clay Stains: To get red clay and grass stains out add about ¼ cup of Cascade dishwasher detergent to your wash along with your laundry detergent.

Grass Stains: Spray the grass stains with pure lemon juice and hang in the sun light. This will work on both white and colored clothes and not discolor your clothing.

Grease Stains: To remove most greasy laundry stains (shirt collars, lipstick, food), apply dish washing liquid onto stain and rub in gently before tossing into washer. A recycled (re- labeled) pull-top water bottle works well as a small container.

Or

To take food grease stain out of a blouse or shirt, before washing put a little bit of talcum powder (baby powder) on the stain and let it set for a day or so, over time the powder absorbs the oil. If the stain still exists, then repeat.

Or

I use carburetor cleaner on all grease spots. Just spray a small amount and it will lift the grease out. I have even used it on a good white shirt with great results.

Gum: Place clothing in the freezer for approximately one hour. Remove the garment and gum will pop right off with fingernail.

Ink Stains: Pour a little rubbing alcohol and then rub a little liquid laundry soap or Dawn dish washing liquid into the stain. Do not use on dry-clean only items.

Ironing: Iron the back of your shirt collar first and the front will iron out flat with no wrinkles in it.

Leather Tennis Shoes: Use a shoe brush and some Barbasol shaving cream then rinse and dry. They will look like new.

Lipstick Stains: To remove lipstick smudges from your clothes simply spray the stain with your favorite aerosol hairspray, then wash.

Mildew: Rub Pine Sol into your garment, let it sit for a few minutes and then wash. Works well with sheets and blankets.

Odor Removal: To remove odors from clothing, add approximately 1-2 cups of white vinegar to the wash. (Works great for baby spit ups and pet messes).

Rust Stains: Make a damp paste of lemon juice and salt. Thoroughly dab the paste on the rust spot, then place the clothing in the sunlight until the paste is dry then wash as usual.

Smelly Clothes: I put 1 cup of baking soda in my clothes, along with detergent then launder. If they smell bad it will take the odor out and it also helps clean them.

Shirt Collar: Dampen collar and rub in shampoo, then launder. What will remove oil and dirt from the hair; will also remove it from the collar.

Softer Sweaters: When laundering sweaters use shampoo, rinse and then add conditioner, and then rinse again. The fabric stays soft longer and with no static when taking it on and off.

Socks: Hate to sort socks? Constantly missing just one? Purchase laundry garment bags, the mesh kind with zipper or draw strings. Have each family member put his or hers own socks in a bag. When there are enough, toss bag in washer, then dryer and then give back to their rightful owner.

Difficult-to-Clean Items: For items that cannot be washed such as heavy jackets and hand-woven quilts that get musty and otherwise unpleasant smell: Fill a spray bottle with vodka and apply to the article. Don't douse the garment, just spritz all over. Any vodka works, and the smell dissipates as soon as the liquid dries. I'm not sure about color fadedness, so test on a small unseen corner before using all over. This method is use on Broadway when costumes often can't be washed at all.

White Socks and Underwear: Use a dishwasher tablet or the liquid dish soap. Use the hot setting on your washer and put your articles of clothing in and run the cycle.

Whites (looking dirty): Use ½ cup of baking soda and ½ cup white vinegar. Run lots of water and pour baking soda and vinegar in water along with detergent. Mix together, and then add the clothes. It will take the iron deposits out.

Or

If you get a stain on anything of "White" colored material, just cut a lemon in half, squeeze out the liquid on the spot. Work the juice into the material then add a bit of liquid detergent. The stain will be gone.

Stain Removal

Blood: Pour a few drops of peroxide on a cloth and proceed to wipe off every drop of blood.

Crayon: Use a damp cloth dipped in baking soda. Comes off with little effort, just a little elbow grease that's all.

Ink in clothes: Even if you didn't realized it until your clothes were launder and dried, the use of Spot Shot works to get ink out of clothing. Just spray the clothing and wash as usual.

Red Wine: Red wine stains will disappear if soaked in white wine.

Soda: Any brand of baby wipes does the trick.

Chapter IV
Miscellaneous

Miscellaneous

Affordable Colored Linens: Since colored bed linens cost more, wait for department stores to have their linen sales, purchase white linens and then dye them your favorite color. You will need to purchase 2 boxes of Rit dye per 1 sheet set.

Air Freshener: To make your own air freshener, mix 2 parts liquid Downey fabric softener to 4 parts water, put in spray bottle and your home will smell great.

Or

Spray your favorite perfume on your light bulbs, and turn on the lights. Also try a little of your perfume on your curtains and then open the windows, makes the whole house smell great.

Animal Care: If you are having problems with your puppy or dog chewing, I suggest using "Vicks Vapor Rub". Rub some of this onto the surface that you want your pet to avoid, the smell of it usually keeps their sensitive noses far enough away that chewing isn't an option.

Animal Control: Pour a little bleach on your outside trash in order to keep the animals away.

Ants: Instead of buying ant killer. Purchase a box of saltine crackers. Crumble the cracker and sprinkle over the ant pile. The salt in the cracker will make the ant explode.

Or

For ants, sprinkle cinnamon along the doorways, outside windows sills, and other openings to the house. It's like an ant shield.

Or

For problems with ant piles just pour bleach all over the pile. This will not only kill the ants, but keep them from coming back. Also you can fill a spray bottle with alcohol and treat the infected area in and around your house. Then, sprinkle baby powder over treated area. This will not only kill the ants, but prevent them from coming back.

Bee Stings: In a mixing bowl add 1 cup of baking soda and ¾ cup of white or apple cider vinegar. Mix until a paste is formed. Tear off a section of brown paper bag (the size of the infected area) soak this piece of brown paper bag in the mixture of baking soda and vinegar. Apply a thin coat of mixture on the infected area, then cover area with soaked brown paper bag. This works best if applied immediately after being stung.

For bee or wasp stings, spider bites, etc. make a paste of plain meat tenderizer and water. Apply to the sting and cover with a Band-Aid to keep in place. The meat tenderizer will break up the protein in the venom and the swelling and pain will soon be gone.

Bleached Hands: Simply use pure lemon juice and add a sprinkle of sugar. Rub hands together vigorously and rinse. No more smelly hands.

Broken Light Bulb: Use a small potato and make sure light switch is turned off. Place potato against broken light base and unscrew counterclockwise.

Bruises: In the event you find you have a bruise try this: Slice a raw onion and place it on the bruised area (avoid broken skin). Allow the onion slice to set for at least 5 minutes and you will notice the bruise heal quicker.

Bug Bites: When camping, hiking, or just hanging on the patio, and you're bit by a mosquito, put Hemorrhoid Cream on it. It will instantly stop itching. Just a little dab will work perfect. Does exactly as it claims: shrinks swelling, stops itching.

Wrap raw salty bacon around bites overnight. It will pull the poison out of the bites.

Bug Repellant: When outdoors put a dryer sheet hanging out of one of your pockets, it will help keep the mosquitoes away. Also works great keeping your TV screen dust free.

Or

Take a paper towel and soak it with vinegar and rub on arms, legs, etc. Once dry it will not smell.

Or

If you have problems with fruit flies, pour a small amount of lemon scented ammonia in a glass and place it in the windowsill. Drives the fruit flies away every time.

Bug Repellant (for flour containers): When you put flour in a container, place a piece of spearmint gum in the container to keep the bugs away.

Burns: Take instant tea granules and add enough drops of water to make a paste. Put over the burned area and let dry. Leave on for as long as possible. It helps heal your burn and ease the pain with the burn.

Burnt Tongue: If you burn your tongue on something hot to eat or drink, put a teaspoon of sugar on your tongue and hold your tongue against the roof of your mouth and let the sugar melt. This will keep your tongue from getting sore from the burn.

Candles: To remove scratches on CD's, rub smooth peanut butter on the CD then wipe it away with a coffee filter.

Canker Sore: For canker sores on the outside of your lips mix baking soda and water to a paste and put on the canker sore. Let harden and leave on as long as possible. This helps dry out the sore and shortens the length of the canker sore.

Car Odor: A great way to get those unwanted smells out of your vehicle is to take 3 or 4 fresh apples and cut them in half. Place in an open container in your vehicle for a day or so. The smell will be gone.

Conserving Energy: To save energy, make sure that in the summer when the air conditioner is running the most during the day the pool filter is running at night and in the winter when the heat is needed at night the pool filter is running during the day. This also works well with a Jacuzzi. This is even more important if you have a load controller.

Dentures: After removing your dentures (or other dental appliance), soak in warm water overnight by adding a drop or two of bleach. Rinse well in the morning before brushing. Not only does it leave your dentures pearly white, but also it kills any fungus that can cause bad breath, mouth sores, and infections.

Diaper Rash: Boil 3 or 4 (dark green) lettuce leaves in enough water to cover them. After boiling the leaves drain the water into a jar or dish with a lid and throw the leaves out. Use boiled juice when cool on baby bottom, rash should be on the way to recovery in 24 hours or less. A local doctor had this tested and still couldn't find out why it works.

Drain Cleaner: Pour 1 cup of salt and 1 cup of baking soda into the drain followed by 3 quarts of boiling water down the drain. Normally this will open the drain immediately.

Dryer Lint: Try using a back scratcher to remove it.

Foggy Eyeglasses: In the winter, if you put a drop of liquid dish soap on your eyeglasses (both sides) and then wipe off with a dry cloth, they will not fog when coming into a warm room from the cold outside.

First Aid: Any time you cut your hand, finger, or any other part of the body, take a spoonful of sugar and sprinkle it in the cut. If you are bleeding, this will thicken the blood and will take the pain away.

Gum in the Hair: Butter will dissolve it so you can get it out faster.

Hair Clarifier: For really soft shiny hair, mix 1 tablespoon of baking soda with 2 tablespoons of your regular shampoo. Leave on for a minute or so then rinse one more time with a small splash of vinegar.

Heartburn: 1 tablespoon of distilled vinegar will provide almost immediate relief (within 5 minutes) of heartburn for weeks.

To get rid of hick ups take a teaspoon of Grape Jelly (not jam). For infants, just dip your finger in the jelly and let them suck the jelly off your finger, for toddlers ¼ teaspoon and children ½ teaspoon. Adjust accordingly to fit your own needs.

Homemade Flea Repellant: Orange peels can help combat fleas and mosquitoes. Collect peels from citrus fruits and keep them frozen in a plastic bag until you have collected about a half a pound of them. Boil the peels in 1 quart of water. Then allow the peels to sit and cool. Then strain the peels and pour the left over fluid into a spray bottle and mist your dog before he goes outside. Mosquitoes hate it, fleas die from it, and it is safe to use. You can also spray their bedding and all around the house for doggy odors as well. It also neutralizes dog and cat urine odors.

Ice Packs: For a quick ice pack, keep a bag of green peas in the freezer and be sure to mark it so you can refreeze it again. The peas in the bag will conform to almost any body part and are not as messy as ice.

To make a homemade ice pack, take equal parts of water and

alcohol in a zip lock bag. Lie flat in freezer until needed. The mixture will be like a really thick slushy.

Itchy Bug Bites: For chigger bites or mosquito bites use Preparation (H) Ointment. It stops the bites from whelping up and the itching.

Fire Starters (Barbecues/Camp): Half-fill each section of a cardboard egg carton with dryer lint; then pour melted wax over it and allow the wax to harden. Cut apart segments for fire starting. Do not use plastic foam egg carton, they will not burn away and they give off toxic fumes.

Fire Starter (Kindling): Save money by making your own kindling for the winter months. Save your toilet tissue and paper towel cardboard rolls. Fill them with the lint trap in your dryer.

Flowers: Place a penny in a vase of drooping tulips and they should stand upright again.

Grass: Get rid of the grass that grows in the cracks of your sidewalk by spraying it with white vinegar. The weeds will be dead by the next day and you can easily pull them out and throw them away.

To remove grass and weeds between sidewalk bricks and along the edges of your sidewalk or home, simply boil hot water and pour it in those spots. It will kill them for the entire summer.

Grocery Store Savings: When a grocery store has an item on sale at a great price, wait and then re-visit the store on the third of seven day of the sale when they are likely out of stock and get a rain check. That way, you can buy it later at the sale price whenever you get ready.

Heating Pad: For aches and pains, take a bag of uncooked rice and put it in a sock. Tie the sock up at the end and put it in the microwave and heat for however long you want it. Pull it out and put it on your ache or pain. Believe me, it works and will save you money too.

Labels for Potted Plants: Slats from vinyl mini blinds can be cut into strips about 5 or 6" long, made pointed on one end and used to label potted plants or seed trays.

Leaky Flower Pots: Simply put coffee filters (usually 4 or 5) in the bottom of the flowerpot when transplanting, it will keep dirt from running out the holes in the bottom when you water.

Lice: For treatment of head lice, take one part white vinegar and one part cooking oil and mix together in a spray bottle. Spray on the hair and work into scalp and hair. Wrap hair with saran wrap and leave on for 1 ½ hours, then use a fine tooth comb to pull out nits. Wash hair well with regular shampoo afterwards.

Mattress Odors: If you have children who have wet the bed and can't get the smell out, place 3 or 4 dryer sheets under the sheet on top of mattress. It covers the odor and smells like fresh laundry. Also works well on smoke smells.

Mailing Boxes: Instead of writing over a logo, using mailing labels, or wrapping over your box of Christmas goodies to go through the mail. Turn your used box inside out and tape/glue it back together. It is easier and nicer looking to use the clean surface of the inside of the box.

Mice: Place cotton balls soaked in liquid peppermint in areas where the rodents are known to come in. Those already in the house will leave and no new rodents will come in.

Mossy Roof: Liberally sprinkle laundry detergent powder along the roof line. A light rain will do the rest.

Moving Clothes: Take a bed sheet and spread it out, grab a handful or two of clothes (leave them on the hangers) then wrap them with the sheet, grab the ends and go.

Nail Fungus: Use Vicks Vapor Rub. Just smooth it on the infected nail. It is fast working and the best.

Paint Fumes: When painting an interior room, mix 1 teaspoon of vanilla per gallon of paint to mask paint fumes.

Paint Removal from Skin: Use Skin-So-Soft spray it will take the paint right off.

Sewing: Put a flat refrigerator magnet in your sewing box, then when your pins spill, the magnet will collect them for you before you noticed they were gone.

Shoeshine: To make a dull hard surface shoes look new again, wipe with Armor All.

Splinters: When you have a splinter, use duct tape to remove it. Make sure you press it on your skin firmly and remove it quickly in the opposite direction it went in. Works well on kids that are skittish to tweezers.

Stop Static Cling in Hair: If your hair has static cling in the winter, rinse your hair in Downy instead of your normal conditioner. It gets rid of the static cling and feels and smells good. Also works well to rinse your hairbrush with it to.

Squeaky Hinges: Spray some Pam cooking spray on the hinges (both sides), wait 5-10 minutes and wash off anything left behind. No more squeak.

Or

Shaving Cream helps noisy door hinges.

Or

Old fashion Pledge in the spray can works wonders on squeaky hinges.

Stuck Doors: Wooden doors that swell or are hard to open and close, try rubbing bar soap along the edges of the door to ease the opening and closing of the door.

Sunburn: When sunburned, rub vinegar on the burn. It will take the burning out and in most cases prevent peeling.

Or

If you have sunburn, rub a tomato on it and it will relieve the burn.

Swimming Pools: For those people who have an above-ground swimming pool and are plagued with birds and all the mess that they make around the pool. Simply take an old black belt and lay it beside the pool. Birds are afraid of the belt and what it looks like and will not come anywhere near the pool. You have to try it to believe it and it works like a charm and to confuse the birds even more, change the shape of the belt occasionally around the pool.

Tangled Cords: Simply use an empty cardboard toilet paper tube and insert the folded cord in the tube and label each. You can then stack them in the drawer and no more tangled mess.

Ticks: If a tick head gets stuck under your skin, make a equal mix of honey and baking soda, mix warm (do not burn skin) and put on a Band-Aid/compress. Leave this on for a couple of hours may need to repeat with heat and ticks head will come out.

Vomit: Spray with Air Freshener, or sprinkle cat litter on it. Cut a paper plate in half, double bag two plastic grocery bags and have beside the vomit. With each side of the paper plate in each hand join them together beneath the vomit, a perfect scooper without any falling out... then move into the plastic bags to be tied and thrown away. Next use more plastic bags as rubber gloves to clean the residue or remove any remaining particles and your hands never touch the matter.

Wallpaper Removal: Brush on fabric softener and the wallpaper will peel off. If you have zippers that are sticking, run a lead pencil up and down the zipper (both sides) several times, the graphite in the pencil will make zipper much easier to pull up and down.

Wasp: To remove wasps and wasp nests, use a wet-dry vacuum to vacuum pest safely into the canister. This is also environmentally friendly.

Notes

Notes

Notes

Notes

Notes

Notes

Notes

Notes

Notes

Notes

Notes

Notes

Notes

Notes

Notes

Notes

Notes

Notes

Notes